For Beautiful Angela, who inspired me.

Dr. David Hill, for the assignment that changed my life.

You...because I want you to feel love and to walk in freedom.

AN ADLERIAN APPROACH TO

SELF-CONFIDENCE

PEOPLE TELL ME I'M AMAZING
BUT I NEVER FEEL GOOD ENOUGH

WORKBOOK FOR HIGH ACHIEVERS

Cover Design & Book Design by Polly St.Onge. Polly Graphic Design, Inc.
www.pollygraphic.com

PART OF THE RELATIONAL GENIUS SERIES

Learn more at RelationalGenius.com

FIRST EDITION

RELATIONAL
GENIUS
www.RelationalGenius.com

TABLE OF CONTENTS

SELF-CONFIDENCE

ACCORDING TO ADLERIAN THEORY

If I had a superpower, I would want to give each person worldwide a deep and profound knowledge of their value. I'd want to magically heal the wounds that originate from bad experiences. Most of all, I'd want people to walk in freedom, knowing that they are unique and wonderful and that they have the right to show up in any relationship or situation as their best selves, without dumbing themselves down or making themselves into someone else's idea of "good enough."

The Adlerian theory provides a framework for how people develop difficulties with self-confidence. Alfred Adler, the psychologist at the center of the framework, is often known for concepts such as Inferiority Complex, Birth Order theory, Social Interest, and Family Constellations.

Adler's theory about self-confidence resonated with me personally, and I later found it useful in conceptualizing the struggles of my high-achieving clients. The theory helps people understand how they developed problems with self-confidence. Thus, this workbook breaks down the theory into manageable bites and guides people through questions about their own belief patterns.

Over the years, I've noticed a high level of interest in self-confidence, regardless of the setting—more website clicks, more questions, and more requests to help build one's confidence as a leader.

YOU'VE got this

When assessing the subtitle for ***Relational Genius: The High Achiever's Guide to Confidence in Leadership and Life***, two of my clients adamantly voted to keep the word "confidence.' Interestingly, they were two of the most successful, high-performing leaders I know. From the outside, no one would suspect that they struggle with confidence. To me, this is the crux of the matter for High Achievers. Struggles with confidence are outside of external successes, position, salary, or praise. I've heard the same thought process from people with High Achieving personalities, regardless of their socioeconomic status.

Thus, this workbook is intended to help people who continue to feel deficient regardless of their accomplishments. It gets to some root questions that can be tough to answer. Answering the questions may create emotions that are messy and hard to feel. I'm not promising that it will be easy, but I am promising that it's worth it.

Dr. Tricia

Break the Rules

BREAK THE RULES

AND MAKE IT YOUR OWN

Christine bought my ***Relational Genius*** book, the 350-page edition with several parts. She told me she'd waited a long time to read it because she wanted to read it from beginning to end, the "right" way. I heard similar comments from other High Achievers. The feedback made me sad because I'd written the book to adjust to the pace of life, where one can flip to the section they need without reading or re-reading the whole thing. I knew that in waiting to read it the "right way," High Achievers might miss critical information at the back of the book.

You might be wired similarly to get things right…which usually means doing things 100% perfectly. For this workbook, the 100% perfect way to use it is in a way that works for you. Maybe there is a question that feels too hard or confusing, and you want to skip it. Perhaps you simply want to think about an answer without writing it down. I believe that if you adjust the way you use the workbook to wherever you are emotionally, it could change your life.

Some elements of this workbook may resonate strongly with you and others won't quite click. Instead of trying to mold yourself around the workbook, mold the workbook around you. Perhaps a section makes you think of a problem in your confidence, and a question springs to mind that gets to the root of your issue. Ask yourself that question and answer it. Maybe there is a concept that doesn't ring true for you, but it makes you think of something else that hits deep in your heart and gut. Focus on the latter.

I'd like you to use the process of completing this workbook as

Your First Exercise in Self-Confidence—

Respond in the way that <u>feels best</u> for you instead of how you feel you <u>should</u> respond. Break the rules and make them your own.

I feel like I need to follow other people's rules because:

YOU ARE

amazing

I will make this workbook my own by:

WHOSE VOICE
WILL YOU
LISTEN TO
IN ORDER TO DETERMINE
Your Worth?

A LOGICAL LEAD-IN TO CONFIDENCE

WANTING TO BE GOOD ENOUGH

Brian wants to be good enough. He's always felt not enough. Brian's brain is an exquisite spreadsheet of logic, and his biggest frustration is that he can't logic himself out of emotion. I'm the first to say that logic often has little impact on emotion, but I want us to start with some analytical questions.

When we struggle with confidence, we've somehow adopted a viewpoint of what is "good enough." Sometimes people have told us what "good enough" is and that we are failing. Sometimes, we arrive at a perception of "good enough" on our own.

One of the elements in Freud's theory of self is the concept of the Superego. It means our sense of conscience and the part of ourselves that judges ourselves. You know how you live in the moment but then part of you judges your actions and reactions to that moment? The judgmental part is the Superego. From this viewpoint, we might judge what is "good enough" from what we read, what people have said to us, and what we've seen in others. One time I wrote down my version of "good enough." It was a fantasy—void of human idiosyncrasies and frailty. It was a pristine and perfect picture of existence that no one could achieve within this lifetime. If I'd decided to judge myself according to that definition, I would have felt like a failure, every day, for the rest of my life.

• • • • •

1. When do you judge yourself harshly?

2. What is your version of "good enough?"
What makes you "good enough?"

3. **Who do you believe sets the standard of "good enough?"** Is it your neighbor, religion, parent, or friend? Who has the final authority on what is "good enough?"

4. **Whose opinions do you listen to about whether you are "good enough?"** Even if you don't think they have final authority, who are the people in your life that influence your self-image?

Heads up—If you said that your opinion is the most important one, this next question will be especially fun.

5. **Good enough for what?** To exist? To do a job? To own space? To have a voice?

6. **What is your core belief about where value comes from?**

What makes OTHER PEOPLE valuable in the first place?

What makes YOU valuable?

DO NOT MAKE

assumptions

ABOUT WHAT PEOPLE THINK OF YOU.

IT IS A CONFIDENCE KILLER AND YOU ARE USUALLY WRONG.

ADLERIAN THEORY

THE BASIC MISTAKE

When I was four, my mother and sister weighed me. I remember standing on the scales and hearing one of them say, *"She's gaining too fast."* They didn't disparage or ridicule me, but I remember thinking, *"Something is wrong with me."* This was my Basic Mistake. The prefrontal cortex of my young brain wasn't developed, so I could not think critically about the comment, understand what it meant for my body, or, most importantly, separate it from my identity as a person. Critical thought helps us process information accurately as adults, but as children, we ingest comments and make meaning of them through a basic lens. My Basic Mistake was the beginning of my belief that I was "other" …somehow deficient from whatever normal was.

It wasn't my fault that I made the Basic Mistake. I was four years old. No one was even being mean to me at that point. **Our Basic Mistakes aren't our fault**. It's just Adler's term to reflect the simplicity of thought process that all children have.

Here is another example.

Bob grew up in a family where manual skills like carpentry were highly valued. The family culture believed it was a good way to earn a living and a reflection of masculinity. Bob didn't care about learning the skills. He was okay at figuring out wood projects but preferred to be inside reading or researching things online.

Bob's father and brothers teased him, saying they needed to figure out a way to "toughen him up" and do "real man's work." Bob felt embarrassed that he didn't quite measure up. He felt deficient in his family and different from the other boys his age.

As a child, Bob had biased information about what makes a person valuable, and he developed a self-schema around it. His Basic Mistake was using partial information to make a larger determination about himself and how the world works.

• • • • •

1. How old were you when your Basic Mistake happened?

2. Where were you?

3. What did you believe?

4. If you had your adult brain, how might you have been able to process the information differently?

WHO
Hurt You?

THE GENERALIZATION OF THE BASIC MISTAKE

Often, although we don't know why, a child's mind doesn't stop with the injury of a Basic Mistake. Perhaps, because of early brain development, the thought that develops is *"something is wrong with me"* rather than a critical analysis of the specific comment.

For example, as a 4-year old, I didn't have the cognitive abilities to think, *"My weight is increasing faster than it should for my age. What foods are my family eating, and what needs to change?"* All I knew was that something was wrong, and it made me feel bad about myself. I felt anxious and embarrassed but didn't know how to process those feelings. (Children can identify angry, sad, and happy emotions, but the more complex ones are tough to navigate, even as adults).

Similarly, Bob couldn't think, *"My family values carpentry, but if I were in a different family who values knowledge, they would praise me."* He felt embarrassed and less than other boys, but he didn't have enough experience to put the feedback into a larger perspective. **Because of this lack of information, he began noticing all the other ways he didn't measure up.** Bob began noticing that his voice differed slightly from the other boys his age. He also noticed that he didn't kick the soccer ball as well. Bob liked his clothing to be ironed neatly, but he felt a little dumb when he noticed that other boys didn't care about wrinkles.

Often a child moves from feeling flawed about one thing to an awareness of other perceived shortcomings. These perceived shortcomings are often fueled by comments from parents or peers, both extremely influential in the development of self-esteem and self-confidence. **As children, our perception matters, not the other person's intention.** Numerous people recall early memories by saying, *"I know this person didn't mean anything by it, but s/he/they said ___, and it stuck with me."*

• • • • •

1. **What other comments or criticisms do you remember people saying?**

2. **Which of those comments did you believe?**

3. Which of those comments do you now see as lies (or inaccurate)?

4. Which of the lies do you still believe about yourself?

WHAT WOULD YOU DO **DIFFERENTLY** IF YOU ***Believed*** YOU WERE AS GOOD AS OTHER PEOPLE?

ADLERIAN THEORY

INFERIORITY COMPLEX

Over time, the generalization of the Basic Mistake to other feelings of inadequacy can morph into what Adler calls an Inferiority Complex. An Inferiority Complex is an overarching belief that one is fundamentally less than everyone else. It is important to note that the Inferiority Complex is unrelated to skill sets. In fact, the more a person has successfully compensated for their perceptions of inadequacies, the higher the discrepancy between how they feel about their personal value versus their performance value. For example, one of the most common comments people make on this topic is, "Dr. Tricia, I have this weird dichotomy about myself that I don't understand. On one hand, I know that I'm better than everyone else at achieving ___, ___, and ___. Usually, I'm the best. But on the other hand, I feel like I'm not good enough and that something is wrong with me.

Bob continued to notice many ways he was different from his family and peers. Adler noted that the Basic Mistake impacts how we make sense of information. We develop a schema of taking in and organizing information. The Basic Mistake alters how we perceive interactions, and the biased information fuels the Inferiority Complex. He called this larger way of adapting to life a Lifestyle; but today, we might call it a Worldview. However, the focus is more on ourselves and our interaction with the world rather than politics and values. Further, we don't consciously choose the Lifestyle; it's a belief pattern that evolves, and we may not realize that we have a choice about it until much later in life. Bob's overall assessment was that he was fundamentally inferior to everyone around him. He didn't notice how he was the same or better than everyone else. He attributed positive relationships or events to luck or chance. If other people spoke well of him, he questioned their judgment. What he believed as truth was that somehow, he was inferior.

Some people live with an Inferiority Complex for a long time, and it can be scary to think about changing it. Even if a Lifestyle is negative and makes us sad, we know how to predict and make sense of the world within that framework. The goal for internal confidence reminds me of other life objectives like happiness or positive relationships. Everyone wants those things, but if they've never had them, there is a vague sense of unease about the unknown. Pursuing internal confidence, happiness, or only positive relationships can be overwhelming because they have no clear definition, path, or guaranteed outcome. Thus, people succeed most by poking holes into the Inferiority Complex and questioning its veracity. The change is gradual, and people can adapt as they go. If this is you, you'll have time to adjust, and it won't be scary. It's like other types of healing. If a person has an athletic injury or muscle pain, there can be a tedious course of rehabilitation with ups and downs. Often it feels like three steps forward and two steps back. Over time, things change, and then one day, a person becomes aware they no longer have pain.

• • • • •

1. Why do you think you are fundamentally inferior?

2. Whom do you see as intrinsically superior to you and why?

3. What has your Inferiority Complex cost you?

4. Are there any payoffs to feeling fundamentally inferior?

Does it protect you in some way?

What are the downsides if you no longer feel inferior?

5. How do you feel about the possibility that you may be just as good/cool/valuable as other people?

WHAT DO
You Feel
YOU NEED
TO
PROVE?

SOCIAL COMPARISON

A DETOUR INTO SOCIAL PSYCHOLOGY

Social psychology is the study of groups and how our social surroundings impact our self-concept. A key concept from the field of social psychology is that of social comparison. Downward social comparison makes us feel better, *"at least I'm not as bad as Sam."* (It might make us feel judgmental, but it still bolsters our self-esteem). Upward social comparison occurs when we perceive others to be better than us. *"Why can't I be more like Lisa?"* It makes us feel bad.

Upward social comparison is a sneaky and evil phenomenon that feeds into an Inferiority Complex. It can help people aspire to be better, but for High Achievers struggling with inferiority, it normally makes them feel worse.

As a child, Bob compared himself to other boys. He did this on the soccer field, in the classroom, and at family gatherings. He noted how high other boys could kick the ball, how relaxed and carefree they were, and how quickly they jumped into manual labor projects. All of Bob's comparisons reinforced his belief that he was inferior.

As an adult, Bob continued to make comparisons. He began working in white-collar environments but still compared himself to other men who seemed more relaxed, more confident, and "a man's man." He felt especially bad if he made mistakes in his field of expertise or if someone else did the job better.

The problem with social comparison is that there will always be someone better or worse off than you. Even if you advance in your career, a sport, or talent, your new level will produce a new pool of peers for your comparison.

Additionally, most people selectively use the comparisons that justify their existing schema. It's an unconscious process by which the Basic Mistake and resulting Lifestyle create selective comparisons reinforcing our beliefs of not being good enough.

To cut through the social comparison trap, I've often asked myself and others, *"would you trade all characteristics of yourself with the other person?"* Most people do a social comparison and want one aspect of someone else. *"I wish I had his intelligence, her hair, their finances."* But I have yet to meet someone who wants to trade everything. For example, one may wish for another person's financial status but may not want that person's marriage. Another may wish for someone else's physique but wouldn't trade on the personality.

• • • • •

What characteristics do you focus on when comparing yourself to others?

Do these comparisons help you or hurt you?

What attributes of your own would you want to keep and not trade?

WE PROTECT OUR

Self Worth

BY FOCUSING ON ACHIEVEMENT

AS A SUBSTITUTE FOR BELONGING.

ADLERIAN THEORY

COMPENSATORY STRIVINGS

Bob hated the constant feeling of inadequacy. Occasionally, he got praise for his broad fund of knowledge, so he put more and more effort into learning. In high school, he was the "go-to" guy when people couldn't find the answers they needed, so he became the information ninja of online research. His feelings of inferiority didn't go away. He didn't feel equal to or accepted by his peers, but he enjoyed the recognition and praise when people needed his skill set. Thus, he worked hard to be the best in knowledge-based activities.

According to Adler, people build skill sets to compensate for feelings of inferiority. He calls these attempts Compensatory Strivings, and it means exactly that. A person tries to compensate for the feelings of inferiority by striving to be great in various areas. Part of the pay-off, if you will, for struggling with inferiority is that people may work extra hard to be excellent. The skill set acquired may result in professional and financial success or praise. From the outside, people will assume that High Achievers must be confident because they are successful. However, many of them have become High Achievers because of Compensatory Strivings.

The background on Compensatory Strivings drives many discussions of the payoffs for painful beginnings. Many people say, *"My childhood was really hard, but it made me work harder, and that's why I'm here today."* One of my clients asked me how much pressure turns coal into a diamond. There are many stories of people who are bullied, abused, or outcasts turning things around from sheer determination to prove others wrong. My response is that sometimes pressure turns people into diamonds and sometimes makes them commit suicide. Most people are somewhere in between, with cracks and scars that make life more difficult. Overall, the Inferiority Complex may hold people back from success, even as they develop skills to cope with it.

If we mix theories of psychology, Compensatory Strivings are a coping mechanism. The focus on compensating helps a person cope with feelings of inferiority. A foundational truth in psychology is that coping mechanisms have their place. They help people survive and deal with both small and big traumas. Coping mechanisms can help a person adapt to a stressor for many years. At some point, though, the coping mechanism loses its usefulness and becomes a separate source of pain.

For example, a child who grows up in an alcoholic household learns to be hypervigilant to the mood changes in others and to adjust his/her voice and behaviors to keep things calm. As an adult, that same child finds it difficult to speak up in work situations where his/her opinion or self-advocacy is critical to outcomes. Thus, the coping mechanisms that protected her as a child make her liable to be viewed as passive or a push-over as an adult. As a High Achieving adult, she may be hard on herself for being a pushover, but it's not her fault. She used a coping mechanism that helped her survive for years, so it will take time for her neurology and emotions to develop a new response pattern.

In the same way that coping mechanisms outlive their usefulness, Compensatory Strivings become a problem when a person has achieved success but feels no joy or peace. Rather than being able to own and enjoy their accomplishments, they continue to strive because the battle against the Inferiority Complex is ongoing. Over time, these strivings challenge the ability to hold healthy boundaries. People struggle with work-life balance because compensatory strivings result in prioritizing activities that bring additional validation.

Special note: There is joy in excellence that has nothing to do with inferiority. One can have both confidence and the pursuit of excellence. The **why** becomes different, though. Instead of striving for excellence to prove our worth to ourselves or others, we strive because seeing how far we can go is fun. The threat of failure has much less power because failure no longer represents confirmation of our inferiority. When we have confidence and strive for excellence out of sheer pleasure and challenge, failure becomes a predictable by-product of stretching into unchartered territory. While not pleasant, the discomfort doesn't threaten our personal sense of self.

• • • • •

1. Where have you put your effort in order to feel good about yourself?

2. How do you feel when you succeed in those areas?

3. How do you feel when you fail in those areas?

4. Do you like doing the items you described in #1?

Would you want to do them if you received no internal or external validation?

5. Do you try new things that you might not be good at? Why or Why not?

6. What might you do differently if you were no longer trying to prove your worth?

WHAT DO YOU *Value* ABOUT YOURSELF

APART FROM YOUR PERFORMANCE?

ADLERIAN THEORY

SUPERIORITY STRIVINGS & PERFECTIONISM

Bob really liked the way he felt when people praised his knowledge. He enjoyed their comments that he could find the answers to almost any question. He put a lot of time into developing these skill sets and became the best in his circles. In the same way Bob had generalized his Basic Mistake to an Inferiority Complex, he generalized his Compensatory Striving until he was the best in everything under his control. Even in recreational activities, it was hard for him to be imperfect. In archery, he wanted to hit the bullseye. In cycling, he wanted to beat his previous best times. The difference between these strivings and that of someone highly motivated but without an Inferiority Complex is this: Bob feels ashamed when he is imperfect. He feels like he has fallen short. He is not trying to be the best only for the thrill of competition but also for the sense of additional validation.

The praise and validation for compensatory strivings can be very addictive. Somehow the expectations of oneself continue to rise. Internally, it's not okay for performance to be average or above average; the bar is only excellent. Perfectionism is a bit of an overused term, so whether we call it that or not, there is a tendency for High Achievers to feel like something is not good enough unless they have accomplished it to the very best of their ability. High Achievers don't expect perfection from others, only themselves. In an odd juxtaposition of expectations, High Achievers who have made the Basic Mistake, see themselves as "other," both in being fundamentally flawed AND in being superior. They have compensated to the extent that they are usually the most skilled person in a group and are used to others falling short of that.

Superiority Strivings have a tactical cost that goes beyond the emotional cost. Many items in life should not be done with 100% effort. The saying "anything worth doing should be given 100% of your effort or not at all" is a fatal maxim for High Achievers. For skilled High Achievers, giving 100% may mean hours of extra time without a measurable return on investment. When juggling professional, family, and health priorities, there isn't enough time to give 100% to everything and be a balanced individual.

I have a little story that I hope doesn't alienate you if you hate school. My compensatory and Superiority Strivings were predominantly academically related. For me, doing the best of my ability resulted in A's. When I returned to school for my Ph.D., I'd healed my confidence issues and realized my academic approach was flawed. If I wanted to continue to be balanced and successful, I needed to figure out the amount of effort that satisfied the requirements versus my perception of doing my best. I realized I had no idea how to get a B, a B+, or an A-. I will admit here that a high-achieving friend and I used to give each other moral support if we got an A-, so I had zero practice with working to achieve anything less. Thus, I systematically varied my effort until I understood the difference between grade points. From there, I could decide based on the task rather than my internal defaults. For example, I remember when I knew I'd need to choose between an A on a small assignment or taking a run outside. I'd committed to keeping fitness as a lifestyle, so I did enough to get an A-, and then left for the run. At that point, I was working to please myself, not just the professor. Confidence had allowed me to make healthy decisions instead of the ones that would validate my value. To be transparent, I also still wanted an A in the course, so I ensured that I could get the ultimate outcomes I wanted; I just had a more strategic way of doing it.

While the above story is about academia, I've found that for High Achievers, it translates to professional experiences, leadership expectations, and all other areas of life. The focus on superiority has left little room to be strategic about achieving a unified strategy of health and optimal outcomes.

• • • • •

1. How have you been rewarded for your Superiority Strivings?

2. What is the cost of your Superiority Strivings? Or do you think there are none?

3. How do you *think* about people less competent than you?

How do you *feel* about people less competent than you?

4. **Do you believe that having internal confidence will make you mediocre? If so, what are the pros of that belief?**

What are the cons of that belief?

Do you have a counter-argument against the possibility that it will make you mediocre?

YOU DON'T HAVE TO BE
PERFECT TO BE

amazing

WHAT HAVE YOU
LOST
BY STRIVING
FOR
perfection?

INTERNAL CONFIDENCE

MAY MAKE YOU LESS PERFECT

Even as Bob excelled professionally, he felt a continued void in his confidence. He'd read several books about motivations for performance. Bob began to understand that while he'd always love winning at new challenges, he didn't want to constantly carry the load of believing that he wasn't good enough. He bought a workbook for High Achievers on Self-Confidence and began to work through it. ☺ He broke the rules by not doing it all at once, writing things that weren't perfect, and even chose not to answer some questions! As he gave himself permission to listen to his own voice, he started correcting the Basic Mistake he'd made in believing he was inferior. His shift was very subtle, but he began closing his computer after reading a document three times instead of going to the fourth read to ensure absolute perfection. He started buying clothing that felt best for him, regardless of whether it was completely on-trend for the male fashion of the moment.

When people no longer believe the Basic Mistake and begin questioning their assumptions of inferiority, the need to compensate, strive, and perfect recedes a little. To my knowledge, it doesn't go away, but the reward of the external validation is now challenged by a person's attention to their own wants and needs. You may go for a run, watch a movie, or sleep a little later instead of perfecting your appearance, proposal, or household. I promise you will not trade your brain and motivation at the door; you will still be you. It is difficult to completely reverse years of training and positive reinforcement, even if you want to. However, you may be a little less polished sometimes if you have foundational confidence. You may be excellent instead of stunningly perfect.

Here's the interesting thing. When trying to be perfect or excellent to gain the approval of others, we don't normally show up as our best selves. It's hard to be authentic and integrated while also being superior. The time and energy demand of being superior make us lop-sided, with a strong bias toward the needs and wants of others or the "shoulds" within our own mindset. The wants of others or the performance we think we should pursue may differ from the path that brings out the best in us.

For me, the superior part of what I have to offer and where I have gained validation is when I can impress people with my intellect; the best part of me is this warm, gooey vault of love that flows out of my core being. The warm gooey stuff is from that place of my soul in which I have nothing to prove, no one to impress, and the absolute best opportunity to connect with someone else's heart. If I'm focused on proving my intellectual prowess, I have less bandwidth to be fully present for another person's emotional needs.

• • • • •

1. **How do you feel about being less perfect?** (If you argue that you are not perfect, think about how you feel if you aim for 89% or 95% of your capabilities instead of 100%).

2. Are you willing to trade being perfect for being impactful? How does that choice make you feel? ***(I bet you want both, don't you? ☺)***

YOU HAVE A SPECIAL GIFT
TO GIVE TO
this world

YOU'LL KNOW
YOU HAVE
self-confidence
WHEN YOU LIST
ALL OF YOUR FLAWS

AND STILL
FEEL GOOD
ABOUT YOURSELF.

LIVING IN COLOR

LETTING ALL FACETS SHOW

When we strive to be superior, by our own standards or someone else's, we usually minimize parts of ourselves. It's hard to let people see your flawed, gorgeous, handsome self while simultaneously being impressive in every way. Saying yes to the tattoo you always wanted will offend someone. Saying no to alcohol because you don't like the taste will baffle another. It's hard to be enthusiastic, loving, and daring while also oozing seriousness, gravitas, and calm. If you think this sounds like the axiom that you can't please everyone, it's true. Yet it goes much deeper than that. What are you willing to sacrifice to be true to yourself?

• • • • •

1. List everything that you love about yourself.

2. List everything you want other people to love about you.

3. **List the characteristics of you that are polarizing:** Some people love them and some people hate them. Can you embrace them?

4. **What will you do to start showing up for yourself?**

I SEE YOU.

You Matter.

LETTING LOVE IN

MY STORY

As noted early in this workbook, my earliest memory of feeling flawed was around age 4, standing on the bathroom scales. My weight increased rapidly as I entered elementary school, and there was another problem. I was part of a religious cultural minority in which we wore head coverings and long, homemade clothing that were out of style. I looked different than the other kids, and I couldn't connect with them culturally because we didn't have televisions or video in our house.

I remember trying to get praise from my mother by doing the dishes at a very young age, but the kryptonite occurred the day I memorized the alphabet backward at warp speed and received a sticker from my first-grade teacher.

From that point on, academic praise and teacher approval was the safe place of my existence. I didn't belong in my school because I was too fat and too religious. I didn't belong in my church because I was too secular and too low in socioeconomic status. I didn't belong in my home because I was too smart and too progressive. I was too much and not enough, everywhere.

Books were my salvation and my sanctuary. I read through the library, gaining borrowing privileges at the middle school library when I ran out of books at the elementary school. Homework was my safe space, and some of my teachers allowed me to work ahead at the next grade level if I ran out of work of my own.

While learning, I desperately wanted to belong. I did make friends, but in that way where it always felt like they were doing me a favor or that we didn't completely connect because of the cultural differences.

In college, I started to feel at home because intelligence was valued. At the same time, my sophomore college year was when I left my church culture. I lost friends, my cultural identity, my reputation, and for several years, a sense of belonging to my own family.

By that point, I was confident on the outside, of a more normal height and weight, socially adjusted, and making friends. I pulled perfect grades and honors. Professors liked me, and peers often said, "I wish I could be as confident as you."

There was one problem, though. The part of me that thought I was completely fine had died on the scales when I was 4 years old, and the bullying from peers, shaming from the religious culture, and lack of fitting in with my family had left me feeling that no one really knew me.

During my Master's program, a colleague, in her pushy and too intrusive way, said, "I know you're always happy, but it seems like there is a deep sadness in you." I was confused and annoyed. I had great conversations and social interactions with colleagues and friends. I got along well with people. I could blend in and converse with people different from me, make them open up, laugh, and trust me. I wasn't putting on an act, so I didn't understand what she thought she saw. Yet the comment stuck with me.

About a year later, I was writing yet another self-analysis paper for one of my psychology courses. By this point, having majored in psychology as an undergrad and in graduate school, I'd analyzed myself so much that I thought nothing was left to learn. I was wrong.

This paper asked us to examine our personalities and incorporate key childhood experiences. I was aware of my own experience growing up but never looked at it from an outside perspective. Seeing the detailed litany of pain triggered a sense of overwhelming compassion for what I'd been through. I remembered all the times I'd been told I was deficient and how

I'd tried to adapt. I remembered that I'd even changed how I laughed after someone had commented on it.

What welled up inside me was not sadness nor pity, but compassion and the awareness that no kid should feel outside in the cold for so long. In that moment, I realized that nothing was wrong with me. What I'd been through wasn't my fault. I hadn't done anything wrong.

My belief about myself and the world shattered. I was stunned, and I didn't know what to do. The epiphany that I was not deficient and deserved compassion instead of judgment wasn't freeing. It was scary. It's like walking confidently along a path in the woods and suddenly being swallowed by thistle with no idea where to turn next.

I called my professor and said, "I know this paper is due in two days, but I had a breakthrough and am completely stuck. I don't know what to do."

He replied, "Don't worry about the paper; come to my office."

I sat there, the darling of the psych department, the academic super-star, utterly unable to explain what had happened. Somehow, he understood.

"Tricia," he said. You have built a very beautiful castle over the years. It is ornate, with gorgeously decorated walls and intricate gates. The walls are very high, and you might even have a moat around your castle for an extra layer of security. The walls have functioned very well to protect you, but they've also kept the inside of the castle rather cold and dark. You let people see the beautiful castle, but you don't open the doors because you are afraid they will judge what is inside. You are afraid to let them in because they might reject you."

He was right. I'd only ever shown people the smart, pulled-together, empathetic side of me. They said things like, "Wow, I can tell you anything," "Here comes Sunshine," and "I need another dose of Tricia because you always make me feel better." Only a few of them realized that I had revealed nothing while they told me everything.

You see, the only thing that equaled my love of people was my fear of them. I'd experienced enough rejection to last a lifetime and didn't want to endure the pain again.

"I get it," I said to my professor. "But I don't really know what to do next."

"You can go slow," he said. "Open the door, just a crack, to the right people. See who is worthy of coming inside the walls. If it feels okay, maybe open the door slightly more."

I did. Little by little, I decided to trust. Little by little, I showed people pieces of myself and watched their reactions. I began by being just a bit more forthright about what I thought and felt, instead of saying what people wanted to hear. I watched for signs of acceptance. Some people stayed in the beautiful courtyard. Some people earned the right to come through the door. For those I allowed in, I practiced opening up instead of putting all of the focus on them to avoid being vulnerable.

Over the next few months, I listened to "True Colors," written by Billy Steinberg and Tom Kelly, and sung by Cyndi Lauper. Silent tears tracked down my face every time it played. The tears weren't of sadness, though. They were tears of healing. And I healed, and I healed, and I healed. The song carries a different message than the one I had believed for so long: being loved BECAUSE of our colors, not despite them, not because we've minimized them. It felt like someone was reassuring me that I was lovable exactly "as is." For the first time, I felt enough.

I opened that castle door further, allowing people to see and love me in whatever form I showed up. It was like someone put a skylight in it, and the castle gradually flooded with light.

Now, the hearth is warm, and the inside of the castle is filled with beauty. Sometimes I get my feelings hurt, but the people who love me help me through it. As a result, my heart is stronger, more flexible, and more confident. I know the risk of relationships, but I also know that the other side of utter rejection is complete acceptance.

Everything I have done since that epiphany has been an effort to see if I can help others recover from the lies that they've believed and see that they are truly lovable. The flash of insight I had from taking one step out and trying to explain my life on paper underlies part of the rationale for this workbook. I'm hoping that if you do the same, some of your negative beliefs will also shatter.

Under every professional engagement that has nothing to do with self-confidence, I watch in case someone needs extra love. I know some castles are very strong, and the walls are thick. I know that opening the doors is scary.

The problem with walls is that they put a ceiling on your happiness. Your life can be as fulfilled as the number of people you allow to love all of you. If you don't let them see the inside of you, you'll always feel the space between them knowing the "real you" and the façade you show them.

You don't have to take down your walls. Maybe you create a door. It's okay to open the door just a crack, to share small vulnerabilities, and to see if people give you the unconditional and nonjudgmental response you need.

With all my heart, I want you to consider that maybe, just maybe, you are beautiful and lovable because of who you are, not because of everything you've done or what other people think you should do.

I wish for you to be free from your assumptions of inadequacy, to throw away the constant striving to be enough. I hope you open those doors just a little because your true colors are amazing. You are lovable, and you are loved. You have a special gift to give to this world.

YOU ARE LOVABLE AND YOU ARE

loved

www.ingramcontent.com/pod-product-compliance
Ingram Content Group UK Ltd.
Pitfield, Milton Keynes, MK11 3LW, UK
UKHW021924190726
13853UKWH00002B/827